Stay OR Go

A PERSONAL INSIGHT INTO THE NEAR-DEATH EXPERIENCE

CAROLYN V. REID

Spiritualist/Angel Certified Practitioner

BALBOA
PRESS

A DIVISION OF HAY HOUSE

Balboa Press books may be ordered through booksellers or by contacting:

Balboa Press
A Division of Hay House
1663 Liberty Drive
Bloomington, IN 47403
www.balboapress.com
1-(877) 407-4847

Because of the dynamic nature of the Internet, any web addresses or links contained in
this book may have changed since publication and may no longer be valid. The views
expressed in this work are solely those of the author and do not necessarily reflect the
views of the publisher, and the publisher hereby disclaims any responsibility for them.

The author of this book does not dispense medical advice or prescribe the use
of any technique as a form of treatment for physical, emotional, or medical
problems without the advice of a physician, either directly or indirectly. The
intent of the author is only to offer information of a general nature to help you
in your quest for emotional and spiritual well-being. In the event you use any
of the information in this book for yourself, which is your constitutional right,
the author and the publisher assume no responsibility for your actions.

Any people depicted in stock imagery provided by Thinkstock are models,
and such images are being used for illustrative purposes only.
Certain stock imagery © Thinkstock.

ISBN: 978-1-4525-7303-8 (sc)
ISBN: 978-1-4525-7304-5 (e)

Library of Congress Control Number: 2013907434

Printed in the United States of America.

Balboa Press rev. date: 08/13/2013

I offer my story in
    celebration of
        the spiritual awareness
            and transformation
                that I received on
                    Thanksgiving Day
                        2011

Table of Contents

Acknowledgments

To *God*, with you I can achieve anything. My gratitude goes to the Most High for divine grace, love and peace. Your spirit infuses my heart with joy! I especially send my love to all the *angels* who have guided me on my journey. My love also goes out to my *ancestors*, who watch over me and cheer me on in life.

To my *parents*, words cannot express my profound thanks. Your multifaceted relationship with me transformed me from a child into a powerful spiritual woman. When I think of you, tears of joy overwhelm my very soul.

To my loving daughter, *Aisha*, who is loyal, compassionate and nurturing! I am blessed to have you as a friend and world traveler. I am grateful for your love and support. You inspire me and keep me spiritually aware of God's eternal grace.

To my beloved *Yaw*, we have coexisted together for many lifetimes with this knowledge, my endearing soul mate; I will always be that special person in your life. You are a best friend, a workmate, a partner, a confidante, a thoughtful soul, a true love, a better half, a significant other.

To my *family and friends*, we were young together. We grow old together. We laughed together and we cried together. Nevertheless, the love remains the same in good times and in bad times. From the very beginning of time, we were placed together spiritually. Thanks to all of you for keeping me centered and on my journey.

CHAPTER 1

Transformation

My life's purpose has been more clearly defined and transformed as a result of my spiritual awakening. An awakening, that revealed to me, how I am both a spiritual and a physical being, evolving through the ongoing process of birth, death, and reincarnation. This beautiful enlightenment has propelled me in the direction I needed to go to achieve spiritual balance and my personal aspirations. Before this change, I moved through life feeling that I was being guided but I could not comprehend why, or by whom. Then, on Thanksgiving Day, 11/24/11, forgotten knowledge of God's divine love was rekindled in me by an archangel and the council of angels. Many sacred insights came to light that day.

Spiritual truths were unveiled and once again, I remembered. My revelation on 11/24/11 helped me to realize my purpose in life. My purpose is to tell my story and send love into the universe. To be able to experience a connection with God and the angels is something for which I am humbled and profoundly grateful. I had a near death experience. As I write my story, I know now that my spirit guides such as angels, guardians, and teachers provide my inspiration. It is a miracle to know that I am worthy and blessed, and so are you. We receive gifts of love, peace, and joy from God, who reveals himself in Exodus 3:14 as, "I AM THAT I AM."[1] Spirituality is a very personal journey and we all follow different paths. My path was revealed to me when I heard seven perfect words on Thanksgiving Day.

"DO YOU WANT TO STAY OR GO?"

Little did I know that these seven powerful words would be the beginning of a renewed awareness? These summoning words, "Do You Want to Stay or Go?" thrust me on a mystical journey of rediscovery of my many incarnated lives here on Mother Earth. During that fateful Thanksgiving Day, God and the angels enabled me to experience a glimpse of the spirit world and the power of God's unconditional love. It is a profound gift to be in the presence of an archangel and the council of angels and determine my destiny at that very moment in time. I was given the chance to stay or go. I made the choice to stay. I was able to choose freely to stay without any questions or warnings from the archangel or the council of angels. This pronouncement would later decide which path or paths I would take to determine my destiny. Self-determination lies in embracing our free will.

Overcoming fear, one can act from a place of inner peace, clarity, and insight. These truths are always with us. We need only to search inside ourselves knowing that God is in our hearts and minds.

Angelic beings have always played a role in our spiritual development here on Mother Earth. Their role is to interact with humans to bring messages from God, but they are also given the role of being protectors and guardians too. Hebrews 1:14 states: *"Are not all angels ministering spirits sent to serve those who will inherit salvation."*[2] Archangels are God's go-betweens, sentinels and teachers. Ancestors are our help mates. They can be family members or friends who have gone to the other side.

Throughout my life, angelic beings have presented themselves to me in several different outward appearances. Before my NDE, in my early childhood years around six or seven, a mature female spirit showed herself and tried to communicate by means other than speech. She communicated telepathically. I was too young and my spiritual knowledge was very limited. Because of my forgotten truths, I became very fearful and ran away from her. I wonder what ever happened to her. Would I ever see her again?

All my life I have felt a presence around me. This spiritual presence always guided me in the right direction and kept me on my path. I had forgotten that God, angels and my ancestors play an enormous role in my journey. Some may call this awareness a premonition or instinct. I call these experiences God's divine grace. We are never left alone. The spirit world is always available to us. The doors will open to multidimensional spiritual encounters; a union with the angels allowing us purpose or meaning in life, and for spiritual truths. These truths became very evident to me on that eventful day in November.

CHAPTER 2

The Denial

As destiny would have it, Yaw, my mate of over 20 years, decided not to go to the coffee shop or to his sister's house for Thanksgiving, as planned earlier that morning. Yaw, who would have normally been out of the house at 5 or 6 am, conversing with his buddies at the neighborhood coffee shop, was instead at home in bed with a bad cold and high fever.

Knowing his plans were canceled, we decided to have an informal dinner at home. I was about to go shopping on Thanksgiving Day for turkey with all of the festive accompaniments, because he and I were committed to staying home and relaxing.

Early that morning, I experienced heartburn, fatigue, and discomfort in my throat, side, and back. I thought I had slept on my side and somehow pulled a muscle in my back. My signs of distress were intermittent. I had not yet foreseen the possibility of a major medical crisis occurring. Suddenly, without warning, reservations about going food shopping entered my mind. I dreaded the thought of carrying all those heavy packages in my arms. I needed a cart and I didn't have one on hand. I decided not to get the preparations for our Thanksgiving Day dinner. I was feeling under the weather. Was this divine providence?

In retrospect, my mortal soul was about to embark on a beautiful, Magnificent, life changing spiritual journey. Another intervention in the construct of the spirit world was affecting the outcome of that day's events. I give thanks for what eventually transpired on that day that changed my life and set me on my spiritual path.

As I wasn't feeling well that morning, I went and settled down on the living room couch to rest. I thought, maybe by resting, the soreness would dissipate. How wrong was I? Suddenly after lying down for over three hours, the pain became more intense. Weakness plagued my body. I became very nauseated. This queasy sensation was keeping me from getting needed rest that morning. I lost control over the situation. Concern, fear, and anxiety engulfed my very being. My gut instinct was to get up from the sofa and sit at the kitchen table. However, hysterics set in and without any thought, I started pacing back and forth in the hallway. I walked for what seemed like hours but, it turned out to be only 30 or 40 minutes.

With all my strength I tried desperately not to moan or make any noises that would disturb Yaw. I needed to determine what was happening to me. Throughout this ordeal, I would unconsciously go to the kitchen for water. I was praying that my unexplained symptoms would go away by drinking the water.

What was I thinking? Drinking water and walking made the pain unbearable.

Frantically, I rushed into the bedroom where Yaw was sleeping. I fell down on the bed next to Yaw shouting at the top of my lungs, *"I'm in pain and the discomfort will not stop."* He jumped up from the bed and said, *"What's wrong?* I'm calling for an ambulance." *"No!"* I said. Then without any warning, I began to bring up all the water I had been drinking. Needless to say, the bed and floor became drenched. I had lost complete control. I was irrational, fearful, and terrified of facing the fact that I was undergoing a life altering situation. This life changing event would take place even if I wasn't ready for the experience. I was in total disbelief and detached from all reality. I believe I was in a state of shock. Looking back, in as much pain as I was in, I have to ask myself; *"Why didn't I go to the hospital sooner?"*

Yaw, now looking petrified yelled, *"I'm taking you to the hospital"* *"No!"* I said, *"I'm in too much pain to go and sit in the emergency room for hours."* I jumped out of bed and started walking in the hallway again. I decided to take a hot shower thinking the hot water would minimize the throbbing pain. To my dismay, the pressure tightened, and the pain in my back settled into my chest. Then the pain went to my left arm causing more distress. This aching and throbbing sensation became more penetrating and debilitating. I could hardly put my pajamas on. This led me to call out to my mate, *"I can't take the pain any longer, take me to the emergency room I'm having a ..."*

I became conscious of what was occurring and I took action and went into a survival mode. I wanted to flee from the pain that consumed me. I needed medical assistance as soon as possible. I changed from my pajamas into my street clothes. Yaw said, *"Let's go right now."*

CHAPTER 3

Divine Intervention/ Crucial Moment in Time

We bolted from our apartment at approximately 6:30 P.M. that night. Due to divine intervention, there were only two or three cars on the road at the time. It took us less than 8 minutes to arrive at the hospital. Normally, the trip would take around 25 to 30 minutes. My guardian angels and ancestors were watching over me. With divine intervention, the angels were setting up the opportunity for me to make a crucial pronouncement which would determine the outcome of that day's events, and the rest of my life. At this particular time, I wasn't aware of any decisions I had to make concerning to *stay or go*. Later, I would learn what an impact this involvement of the angels would have on my future. Destiny was about to set the stage for the rest of my life and maybe my future incarnated lives. Had I learned my life lessons or finished my purpose in this life? Only time would tell. I had a simple yet quite complex decision to make and the stage was being set up for this crucial moment in time.

Yaw parked the car right next to the emergency room door. We rushed into the hospital. I looked around the room and there were no patients in the area, only the hospital staff. This was another example of the angels' intervention. This infirmary was one of the busiest hospitals in New York City and the emergency room was empty! Walking at a snail's pace to the nurse's station, I called out, *"I'm having a heart attack, please help me! Get a doctor right away."* The receptionist sat me down on a chair next to her and called for the nurse. The nurse took my vital signs and hurried me into the emergency room where I laid on a gurney moaning and crying, *"Please help me, I need help."*

I began to moan and cry with intensity. Then suddenly I noticed a lady in the next bed. I thought to myself, *"This is an emergency room."* This lady was very sick herself. I said, *"I'm so sorry, I normally don't cry in public, but I'm in so much pain. I can't help but cry."* She replied, *"Please don't worry about me I'm not in any pain. I know you are very sick because I heard the doctors talking to the man who came in with you. The doctors told him, "Please sign the consent forms because she needed to be operated on as soon as possible or she will die."* At that very moment, I heard the doctors coming toward my cubicle.

Two or three doctors rushed to my bed side. One doctor listened to my chest and said, *"You are experiencing a heart attack. We will give you something for the pain but you need x-rays, ultrasound, and blood tests."* After all the tests were performed, the doctor informed me that one of my main arteries was blocked almost completely. Fatty deposits had built up in the walls of my main artery and slowed the blood flow. *"We need to take you to the operating room right away to clear your artery."* But, before the nurses placed me on a stretcher, they asked me to sign the consent forms for the procedure and so I did. They told me that Yaw said, *"Since Carolyn is not unconscious it's best that she signs for the procedure. She's the one who would know best what she wants done to her. If she was unconscious then I would definitely sign for the Coronary Angioplasty procedure."* I was then rushed to the operating room.

In the operating room, another doctor advised me that he would be performing a technique called Coronary Angioplasty. He told me he would carefully insert a thin flexible catheter (tube) in my groin area. This tube had a balloon attached to it that would go up through my blood vessel and open my clogged artery. He also stated, *"You will be awake during this nonsurgical procedure."*

I became frightened, anxious, and needless to say, overwhelmed by the decision not to be put asleep during the procedure. Most terrifying was being unable to see what the doctors and nurses were doing. I felt a sense of frustration. I was frustrated because a beige colored barrier was blocking my view from the doctors, nurses and monitors. Once the doctor inserted the catheter in my groin and up through my vein, I heard him discussing with the other doctors, the location of the catheter. They used numbers to verify the direction and placement of the tube to try to unblock my damaged artery. This realization of being completely helpless and in the hands of someone else was entirely new to me. I felt traumatized by the strange and unwelcome intrusion to my body, but I decided not to resist or complain. This was out of my control and in the hands of God;

and the contract I made before I came back to Mother Earth in this lifetime. Yes, before I came to Mother Earth, I was spirit, living with other spiritual beings and God. I do believe that we decide or chart out our lives before we enter into another incarnated life here on earth or in the universe. I contracted to experience this life-changing event so I would find the meaning or purpose to my new awakening.

Michael Newton, in Memories of the Afterlife, quotes Trish Casimira: *"Life-between-lives regression reveals that relationships with members in our soul group fulfill a contract that was agreed to prior to incarnation. At birth, we agree to forget that arrangement so that we can have the experience without any influence of memory. Even so, amnesic blocks can be removed through hypnotic regression."*[3] I believe that we have free will to decide who our parents, brothers or sisters will be, and where we choose to live. We are not aware of our original contract or even the purpose of being on Mother Earth during our lives. Certain members of our soul family or soul group will be around to offer assistance and guidance to help us to stay on our original course. This enables us to keep our contracts that were made before we incarnated to earth.

CHAPTER 4

The Awakening

This feeling of helplessness unnerved me. I began looking around the room to keep from becoming ruffled. I needed a distraction to settle my fragile nerves. I happened to glance up on my right hand side above the table and ceiling and saw an enormous man in a gray tweed suit. Who was this man? Where did he come from? Why was he here? Why was I the only one to see him? Will I be all right? All these questions made me feel a sense of urgency. What was happening to me? Am I dying? Is he coming for me?

The man in the gray tweed suit was sitting in a gigantic brown wooden chair looking down at me with authority, compassion, and concern. He appeared over 9ft. tall even though he was sitting in a chair that was in open space. I could see he had very wide shoulders. The man in the tweed suit appeared void of human pigmentation. His face was very keen; he was in what appeared as a silhouette or rough image. His hands were gigantic and powerful. His face and hands were gray almost like a stencil or pixel textured appearance. He was not of this world. I could sense he was a gentle spirit. For some reason, I remembered he had on brown shoes with eyelets decorating the front of each shoe. I kept looking at his shoes. I've seen these shoes before but could not place where, or who was wearing these unique shoes.

I looked up again at him. He was looking straight down at me. I still didn't know what was happening but he looked as if he had something urgent to tell me. Before he spoke, feelings of alarm, panic and trepidation entered my consciousness.

The man in the gray tweed suit seemed to be very calm although I wasn't. His calmness made me feel relaxed somewhat but cautious. His demeanor was austere and to the point yet loving at the same time. Because I was in the middle of heart surgery, I got the impression that he was a messenger from God with very important information to reveal to me. I was thinking, *"Please let this be an encouraging encounter."* I sensed his intentions were constructive. His body language was motionless, and at the same time, soft and confident. I still didn't know what to make of this experience. Time and space stood still. I was trying to anticipate what the man in the tweed suit was here to tell me. Suddenly, I stopped thinking and concentrated on him again.

He remained unintimidating and tranquil. I was not afraid of him. In the past I'd felt threatened by a similar experience, and I tried to deny and forget it ever happened. This time I felt a sense of peace, so I did not tell the medical staff what was happening. I waited and listened.

Suddenly, the man in the tweed suit began to speak. *"Do you want to stay or go?"* were the only words he spoke to me. In his calming presence, I did not feel rushed to answer. Somehow, I knew that this was a divine moment in my life. The angel intervened on my behalf to issue a fateful inquiry: *"Do you want to stay or go?"* I knew that he meant to ask if I wanted to stay on earth or return to the celestial world. At that very same time, I heard a group or council of spirits talking amongst each other. This council was located right opposite the man in the gray tweed suit.

At the same time, my daughter, Aisha's face, appeared glowing in color to the left of me in contrast to the black and white apparition of the man. As soon as I saw Aisha's face, I had to stay for her. I had made a promise to God before I gave birth to her, that I would be there for her. She hadn't started a family yet and I didn't want her feeling left alone. Many of our family members had already passed on.

I also knew I had unfinished life lessons to concentrate on. From the point of observing the male angel in the chair, and sensing the other angels sitting in a group across from him, it was apparent I had more to rediscover about the spirit world. I said, *"I want to stay."*

At the same time, I was aware that I was the only one who could make the decision to stay or go. My spirit guides would not be able to make this decision for me. This was my true awakening and I needed to learn more about this experience. With this revelation, I wanted to live, explore and learn why I was given the opportunity to stay. While I was making the decision to stay, I had a sense that a council of angels was there talking amongst themselves. I couldn't make out what they were saying. All the communication occurred through mental telepathy and clairvoyance. No one else in the room could hear or see what was revealed to me. I didn't indicate to anyone in the operating room what events were taking place right before my very eyes. I became oblivious to what the doctors were doing. I had made my decision.

Once I said, *"I want to stay,"* a calmness that was so powerful and magnificent encircled me. Was the reason I wanted to stay already ordained? Yes, I believe so, because things were already put into place for me to stay before I came to Mother Earth. At that very moment, I knew my life had changed forever. Fear had lost its hold on me. I needed this experience to free myself from living on the fringes of life. After the encounter with the archangel, council and Aisha, I needed to focus my attention on what was transpiring in the operating room. I realized that the doctors were still working on my damaged heart.

The doctor performed an angiogram, a small amount of radiographic contrast, a solution containing iodine, which is easily seen on X-ray images, was injected into my blocked coronary artery. The plaque build-up in my artery turned out to be so severe that my doctor decided on medical treatment instead of performing the angioplasty. I knew then that an angel played a significant role in my recovery. Who was this archangel? Could this have been Archangel Raphael (the angel of healing) that was sent to restore my physical and spiritual body? Archangels appear as huge spiritual beings. The man in the gray tweed suit fit the description of an archangel. Doreen Virtue, in The Healing Miracles of Archangel Raphael states,

> *"The term archangel (pronounced ark-an-gel) is derived from the Greek phrase the greatest messenger of God. Arch means the first or the greatest, and angel means messenger of God."*[4]

Archangels are bigger, more dominant, and more specialized than guardian angels. Archangel Raphael's chief role is to support, heal, and guide in matters involving health. He is believed to be one of the chief angels in the heavenly realm. He has many important responsibilities such as healing the sick, protecting animals, and he is also the angel who safeguards us when we travel from place to place.

After the angiogram was completed, I was escorted to the Cardiac Intensive Care Unit (CICU), where my beloved Yaw and Aisha were waiting to greet me. They were distraught and needed consoling. I immediately said, *"I am fine. I am fine."* They both kissed and hugged me. I felt the tension they experienced dissipate at that very moment. I felt calm and less frightened for them because I knew that their spirits were at peace. They needed to see me and that was enough for them. I stayed in the CICU unit for four days and would remain in the hospital for an extra day.

During the second day in the hospital, I experienced many different emotions. First, I felt perplexed because I was unable to acknowledge any warning signs during the onset of my heart attack. All I wanted to do was sleep and not eat anything in the hospital. Second, I was emotionally drained and this feeling was affecting my perception of what had just happened to me. I slept until late that afternoon. When I woke up I felt restored, alive and peaceful. I focused on the vision I had experienced in the operating room. I was smiling from ear to ear.

I kept thinking about the man in the gray tweed suit. Was he Archangel Raphael, or was he my guardian Angel Rachael, who was introduced to me at a spiritual event prior to having the heart attack? Will I ever see him again in this incarnated life time? What effect would this encounter have on my life? Why could I see the spirit angel but not the group of angels sitting at the table? All of these questions were dancing in my head. Suddenly I heard familiar voices in the hallway.

My family members came that evening to visit me. They had a disturbing look on their faces. Looking back, I must have looked fragile, tired, and distraught. However, inside spiritually, I felt joyous, not stressed at all, and uplifted. I smiled and said, *"Looks are deceiving, I feel great!"* A sigh of relief came forth from their mouths. We talked and laughed for hours about our family members' funny mishaps and accomplishments. They left my room with smiles on their faces. I will always give thanks for having a loving and caring family. Before I went to sleep that night, I wondered whether they also were part of the reason I chose to stay. If I had decided to go what impact would this decision have had on my family? We had lost so many beloved family members in such a short period of time. I needed my family as much as they needed me.

The third day, I spent sleeping and not eating again. I was afraid to eat. For some reason, food wasn't appealing or wanted. When the doctors and nurses made their rounds, they stated, *"You must eat something to get your strength back."* Without giving much consideration, I said, *"I'll try."* At this point, I knew I wasn't going to eat anything that day. Why didn't I want to eat? What was happening to me that would stop me from eating? Unhealthy eating and over-eating were two of the primary reasons I had the heart attack.

That afternoon my loved ones came to visit me again. We talked, laughed, and exchanged words of love and expressed appreciation to God, for letting us commune together that night. Then, the question came up again about me not eating. I said, *"I'm not hungry and I'm afraid to eat."* They said, *"You must eat or you will not be able to leave the hospital because you will be too weak to leave."* I said, *"I will eat something tomorrow."* Someone said, *"Yes, but you need to eat tonight."* I replied, *"No, I can wait until tomorrow."* The subject was dropped. Visiting hours were over. They left and I began thinking about the man in the gray tweed suit once again. Was I dreaming when he appeared? No, had I seen him before? Yes, or maybe another archangel or was this archangel the same archangel as before? I had a strange feeling I had seen or felt him before, but was he the same archangel I saw when I was a little girl who appeared as a woman. In the hospital, I had plenty of time to reminisce about my past experience with the angelic realm.

At the age of six or seven I came down with a severe case of pneumonia. My mother, Florence had to quarantine me. She placed me in the living room so she could watch and care for me. I was extremely happy because back then families only owned one TV. I'm proud to say that my father built the TV himself. Back then, the TVs were always kept in the living room. In fact, it was the only TV in the neighborhood. While watching the TV late one night, I witnessed a lady to my right in my parent's living room door. She was encased in an oval frame. I could see blue sky over her head. She had on a green hat, green suit with a white lacy blouse, and a small bouquet of flowers on the left side of her jacket pocket. Her demeanor was very calm, friendly and grandmotherly.

I became frightened. I looked around the room to see if she was a reflection from the TV. No! I looked out of the living room window to see if the lady's reflection was coming from there. No! I was very young so I thought maybe someone was outside the window. However, we lived on the seventh floor in an apartment house. There was no way that someone could have been outside the window. I became so troubled that the lady in green gave me this great big warm smile and said, *"Don't be afraid I ..."*

At that very moment I jumped from the sofa, but then something told me not to go through the oval where the lady was located, but around the oval. I went around the oval and back to my bedroom and proceeded to go to sleep. I never went back to sleep in the living room again. The next morning my mother, said, *"Dale,* (nickname given to me by my loving Aunt Lillie) *why did you decide to sleep in your bedroom?"* I replied, *"I was feeling better, so I just wanted to sleep in my own room."* In those days, I didn't know that my mother had a similar spiritual experience herself. I thought I had no one to talk to who would understand what had happened to me that night. I never heard anyone say they saw an angel nor had an angel talk to them.

This was my secret until now. I know now that secrets are based on fear. Fear blocked my development and stumped my spiritual growth in this lifetime. Before I fell asleep that night, I promised myself, I will never be afraid again. I realized that the lady was not going to harm me. She only wanted to speak to me. I have often wondered what the lady in green wanted to convey to me. I hope one day she will come back and say hello. I do miss her and even to this day I think of her as the first stage in my spiritual awareness.

The morning of the fourth day, I ate half of a small cup of hot breakfast cereal and all of the fruit cocktail. All of a sudden it came to me. I had been fasting for those three days. I was fasting because a miracle had taken placed on Thanksgiving Day. My body needed a period without food so I could become healthy spiritually as well as physically. Fasting helped my body facilitate the healing process. The act itself purified my body and spirit.

Going without food helped me heighten my spiritual growth. Fasting enabled me to focus my energy toward rebuilding self-awareness. It also gave me the opportunity to reconnect with my body and mind. In the future, I will fast to put my body at rest and to connect directly to God. Fasting will provide me with a greater perspective on how I'm living, where my path is leading me, and why I need to take a particular journey.

The afternoon of the fifth day, I left the hospital. I had lost over 23 pounds. I stayed at Aisha's apartment for 5 weeks to recuperate and get my strength back. I realize now, Aisha is an old soul whom I believe was my mother in another life. Our time together seemed so surreal. Aisha devoted all of her non-working hours to making me feel loved, secure and centered. I became the daughter and she took on the role of mother. I'm so proud of how nurturing she has become as a young woman. It was a marvelous and fruitful experience we had together. I will always cherish our special moments during those trying times.

This experience with her reminded me again why it was so important for me to stay. All the doctors before I had Aisha told me I could never conceive a child. They never really told me why or what fertility treatment I needed to undergo to conceive a baby. At the age of 35, I was blessed with Aisha. The doctor said, *"You are pregnant but I don't know how this happened."* I started to say it takes a man and a . . . . I stopped myself because this was too important for me to joke about my pregnancy. However, my entire pregnancy was either spent in bed or in the hospital. I was always in pain and going into premature labor.

The doctors told me several times during my pregnancy, I could lose my baby at any time. Two or three months before my due date, I had a dream. I dreamed I would have a healthy baby girl. I could see her face, size, and how beautiful she was. In that same dream, Aisha was around six years old. She was on a trampoline happily jumping up and down. I was not next to her but at a distance from her. My mother was right next to her. It seems my mother was keeping a watchful eye over her and still is but in a different dimension.

On a beautiful day in July of 1980, an amazing baby girl named Aisha came into my world, raising her head and looking me straight in my face. You could hear a pin drop in the delivery room. Everyone in the delivery room was as shocked as I was. They all were watching the interactions between Aisha and me. It was as if we were sending love telepathically to each other. Everyone in the delivery room was watching how Aisha was responding to me without any words from me. I think they were as amazed as I was with this very special moment between mother and daughter.

Suddenly, everyone in the room smiled and one of the nurses said, *"You have your work cut out for you."* They continued to look after the baby and me. It seems that Aisha wanted to see who gave birth to her. I had the feeling she already knew me. Now looking back, Aisha was always a part of my spiritual journey. She was born so I would stay. The way I expressed my gratitude is by loving her for who she is and will become in the future. In looking back, it occurred to me that the dream I had before she was born came true.

When Aisha turned six, I decided to go back to college. My classes were at night and I worked mornings at the same college I was attending. My mother became Aisha's caregiver during those early developmental years of her life. My mother was a very wise person and I'm so glad that she instilled many spiritual values in Aisha's life as she did in my life. Dreams do come true. Aisha jumping on the trampoline was a divine insight into our future together. She was happy and I was able to pursue a library career. She is my gift from God. We have always been able to communicate our feelings to each other. She is my joy and the reason I'm here today.

I had mentioned the incident in the operating room on 11/24/11 to her but I didn't elaborate. I needed more time to get my thoughts in order. I wasn't mindful of what the full ramifications of the events that took place would be on me. I was waiting to discuss this incident with my mate and Aisha together because I needed their support and input. I didn't want to tell my story twice. I needed to feel centered first, then I would be able to convey to them what changes I needed to make to live a more healthy and spiritual life style. It was time for me to return home. Maybe there I could gain clarity and then be able to tell them my story.

Aisha drove me home. I never got the chance to talk in detail about what took place at the hospital on that faithful day with Aisha or Yaw. During the ten days I was home, I tried a couple of times to communicate all that went on in the operating room. However, for some reason, I felt it wasn't the right time to divulge this information. Yaw and Aisha were still in a state of unrest and needed time to recover from all the trauma of the possibility of losing me. There is always a right time and place for everything. However, this pivotal moment in my life needed to be confirmed, understood and absorbed. I needed validation that a spiritual rebirth had taken place. In looking back, if I had remembered that I contracted these experiences before I incarnated to Mother Earth, fear would not have taken such a hold on me.

I was able to use this time at home to recall other spiritual experiences I encountered over the years. If only I remembered

Mama's NDE, I would have been more prepared for my own spiritual transformation.

My grandmother experienced an NDE in the 1980's. I received a call from my much-loved mother saying, *"Your grandmother* (affectionately called Mama) *is very ill and near death."* My mother insisted we leave home right away to see her. We left from New York City for Leesburg, Virginia that very next day. While driving to Virginia my mother and I talked for hours about how Mama would not want us to be depressed or disheartened. She had always said to the family, *"When my time comes, I will be ready to meet my maker, so don't cry for me. I will be in a better place."* It took us seven and a half hours of driving before we finally reached the hospital.

In the hospital room, my precious Mama was on her death bed with all of her vital organs shutting down. She illuminated the room with her beautiful smile. To my surprise, Mama was singing spirituals that I had never remembered hearing before. She said, *"Can't you see them, can't you hear them,"* I replied, *"No Mama."* Mama said, *"They sound so beautiful"* and she begun to sing, *"Sing with me, Dale."* I couldn't sing with her because this was her moment of spiritual enlightenment and somehow I didn't want to interrupt her experience. I felt this was my grandmother's journey and I was there as an observer and not a participant.

Tears of joy streamed down my face at that very moment. I knew that she was at peace. Mama was going home to be with God, angels and her ancestors. Her last days were with family, friends and the angels. She lived a spiritual life. Her path in life enabled her to give to others and allowed her to be caring, and most of all, loving. Mama was a well-respected and inspirational matriarch in our family and in the community. She was the go-to person for advice. She was never too busy or preoccupied to listen or help resolve family issues. Mama was the most knowledgeable, proficient, and intuitive person in the family next only to my adoring father, Clarence, and my beautiful mother who happened to be my best friend.

Mama transitioned into the spirit world a week later. In my heart, I know that God and the angels rewarded her with a graceful journey home. Miracles do happen all the time. This miracle of seeing and singing with the angels was an example of God's unwavering love for all spirit beings. God's life force energy is in all of creation. It was a gift to have had Mama in my life. I felt God's manifestation and love at my grandmother's bed side and at her memorial. Her coming home celebration must have been exhilarating. I'm certain that all the angels rejoiced and welcomed her back into her cluster (family of spirits) in the afterlife.

Mama would always be with me in spirit, I would never forget her. She was the love of my life, my guardian when my parents were not around, my teacher, and spiritual guide here on earth. All of my creative gifts flowed from her to me. Mama instilled in me her unique sense of style, artistic design, and her inventive ways of preparing foods from all over the world. She was my hero and my creative partner. I give thanks for having her in my incarnated life here on Mother Earth. Our life together was one beautiful dance of creativity, exploration, and love. Her wisdom, grace and steadfast devotion established a bond between us which will last for eternity.

I also pondered on the significance of the seven words, *"Do You Want To Stay or Go?"* I replied with four words, *"I want to stay."* What role did the numbers 7 and 4 play in my life? These four words correspond to four classical elements: Earth,

Air, Fire, and Water. Everything under the sun is composed of these four elements, from which all things come forth, and to which all things will sooner or later return. The four elements demonstrate the unity between physical life and the spiritual dimensions.

Earth is where I need to stay and grow as a spiritual being. I am steadfast in my decision to stay. I have a lot of spiritual work to complete. I have many more things to heal and learn before I return home to the spirit world.

Air is the breath of life itself. It can be the thoughts we send out into the universe. It is also the waves or vibrations of wisdom we communicate to each other and receive from the angels. We do this by using mental telepathy. Air is our spiritual power whether on Mother Earth or of the heavenly realm. It is the all-knowing, the gift we received from God, to use as a tool for living a spiritual life of understanding and growth.

Fire is the element with the highest vibration. It evokes God's oneness with the universe. In the spiritual world, fire is light. Light is energy, intuition, clearing, transformation and is an extremely powerful element.

Water is a symbol of purification. It is the cleansing power representing spiritual rebirth, and inner freedom to choose the path or paths I need to take to complete my journey. Water signifies creativity and the source of the gifts I have received to express my spirituality. Taking the shower on 11/24/11, I know now that the shower itself was part of my rebirth. I needed to take a shower in order to experience my new awakening. This new awareness was received and fully comprehended on Thanksgiving Day and will remain in my heart forever.

Everything happens for a reason. I used these same elements to describe my jewelry business in 1996. My gems, stones or beads are made from Mother Earth. These elements can be motivational for those who wear my jewelry. My line is a reflection of my communication with the spirit world, creativity, and awareness of God, the angels and my ancestors. My jewels for the journey represent my emotions, love, and compassion for all things that possess energy or light. Good or bad situations in life do not just happen. There is always divine order, reason, or purpose in our journey here on earth. My jewelry business keeps me focused and centered. My jewelry making is an expression of my love for God, angels, and my ancestors. This creative ability is a gift from God. I will always treasure this gift.

"Do You Want to Stay or Go?" contains 7 words. My first name Carolyn contains 7 letters and my last name Reid has 4 letters. According to: McGough, Richard Amiel, author of The Bible Wheel Website, *"The root of the number seven means Perfect, Complete, or Satisfied…and the number 4 describes the throne of God as surrounded by a rainbow and precious stones are used to describe the colors of God's throne."*[5] My name was not chosen by chance. My name was a gift chosen before I was incarnated here on earth. Were these observations of the number 7 and 4 just my imagination, coincidence, or divine order? I would like to believe it was divine order. In fact, I do know it was divine order.

Thirty one years after Mama had her NDE; I had a near death experience. The day I experienced my NDE, I refused to accept or believe how sick I really was. Fear has many attributes. I felt angry, anxious and apprehensive. All these attributes played an important role in my lack of responsiveness and ownership for what was about to occur. I felt out of control and helpless.

Mama's NDE was unlike my own near death experience. I stayed instead of transitioning. I bear witness to God's unswerving love. After many days of reflection, rest, and excellent care, my doctors finally agreed I could return to work. On January 2, 2012, I returned to work.

CHAPTER 5

Meditation/Inspiration

When I returned to work, I decided to mention my angelic experience to my coworker/friend who happens to be a college librarian. She said, *"Don't forget to call Bonny."* Bonny L. Hughes, RMT is an Ordained Spiritual Minister and Spiritual Counselor. She's also an Intuitive Healer. *"Please let her know about your experience in the hospital and that you suffered a heart attack on Thanksgiving Day."* I said, *"I will definitely call her tonight and give her all the details. I will let her know, how my encounter with her helped me not to be afraid or in denial of what happened to me that eye opening day that would change how I view the universe and God."*

Before I met Bonny, I was a religious person and not a spiritual being. That is, I believed in God and didn't understand the role the angels and the ancestors had in my life here on Mother Earth. I know now that both religion and spirituality are valuable expressions of love and can be pathways to God. Religion has set guidelines that adhere to a certain doctrine or belief system. There are priests, clergymen and women, rabbis to articulate God's message; whereas, spirituality adheres to the experience of God's love. Meditation is a tool or guide through which each person connects with the spirit world without a mediator. Spiritual people communicate directly with the source which is God. As a spiritual person I believe that Mother Earth and the universe are God's creative energy. They are his very being. God is in all that was and is to be. Bonny presented me with many spiritual facts and tools that change my whole way of thinking about God, fear and love.

I first met Bonny, September 17th, 2011; a friend took me to meet Bonny at her midtown apartment. I needed some insight concerning my future and my friend told me, *"Bonny is the person to talk with."* Before I met Bonny that day, she did a reading and wrote:

> *"Carolyn, release and surrender—When we "hold tight" to problems, fears and angers, we wear ourselves out. By asking the angels for help, we release our hold,-releasing "our burdens" that no longer serve us, we have an open heart, open arms—open spirit to receive.*
>
> *The highest energy there is, is JOY! It opens our being to understand everything is possible. Joy comes when we see, feel, know and appreciate all the gifts*

within each moment. Joy allows you to attract and create your present and future moments in love.

Doors are opening-Now is the time to act on your inspirations. Don't delay or procrastinate. Ask and you shall be given. It's waiting now for you to accept fearlessly."

She also gave me these words of wisdom,

"Carolyn, release your fears and asked the angels to help you through the process." Bonny also stated, *"You are worthy."*

During a spiritual reading, Bonny identified Archangel Raphael and Gabriel to me. She said, *"These are your spirit guides."* She also saw many of my ancestors and my childhood dog, Heidi. The connection was very powerful, fulfilling, and impacted my life in a very positive manner. Now, I make it a habit to converse with my loved ones who passed over into the spirit world. I feel them around me especially when I feel alone or need encouragement. Bonny told me that, "Your *mother and father leave you signs. Your mother offers feathers and your dad leaves coins for you to find."*

Their offerings keep me grounded spiritually and I'm always aware of God's presence when I see these gifts. In addition to leaving objects, my mother comes to me in my dreams. She connects with me when I need a solution to a problem. She lets me know if I'm on the right track or not. I feel content and tranquil knowing my ancestors are with me. My ancestors live with the angels and other kindred spirits. They all watch over me here on earth. Bonny saw the beautiful light my spirit projected from my earthly body. I didn't know at the time, that this encounter with Bonny would set the tone for what would occur on Thanksgiving Day. However, I did feel a transformation that very same day. I felt a sudden shift in my demeanor from being sad to feeling pleased, even happy.

Bonny e-mailed me the next day,

> *"It was such a pleasure to meet you and get to know you a bit yesterday. You have a beautiful Light that shines, let it out!! This is who you are. We can begin to open and change when we become aware of our thoughts, one thought at a time, and release the thoughts that no longer serve us. As you know, the past has no power over us-we take the loving lessons and grow and release all else. The future is not here yet, so we prepare and ask for guidance and we begin to live NOW, in the amazing moment we are in. When we live with an Attitude of Gratitude we feel the shifts begin to happen in all things."*

What powerful words! I so needed to hear them from someone who could articulate what I was feeling in my heart. Bonny gave me a CD, *"Connecting with the Angels"* to meditate with. This very CD opened doors and led me down the road to decode some of my life's truths. This CD also opened me and helped me meditate. For the first time in this life, I was able to silence my mind (ego) and listen to the spirit world. Thank God and the angels above for this wonderful opportunity to experience pure love and be in their presence.

On several occasions, I connected with the spirit world through teleconferences, workshops, and audio tapes. These classes enlightened me and inspired my quest for knowledge. The spirit world opened its doors and allowed me to experience love, peace, and joy in my deepest being.

One of the tools I used was Bonny's sister's (Linda) CD entitled, "Energy Expansion Meditation." Linda M. Martin's is a Doctor of Metaphysics and Ordained Minister, Dove of Light Healing Sanctuary. While listening to her CD, I heard Native American chanting.

After listening to the CD, I remarked to a friend how I enjoyed the CD and the beautiful Native American chant. My friend said, *"There was no Native American chanting on the CD. You were listening to Crystal Singing Bowls only."* A lovely smile broke out on her face. She said, *"You are opening"* (Spiritually connected or conscious). She became very interested in my story and encouraged me to read books on Spirituality and how it related to my extraordinary break through into the spirit world. This remarkable incident would channel me on a path that would alter my life forever. Thanks to Bonny, Linda, and my friends, through counseling and encouragement, I was able to decide which path I needed to take. They helped me pave the way to my spiritual growth and development.

I started buying and reading books and CDs that specialized in the spirit world. By pursuing my interest in Spirituality, I'm able to experience many spiritual insights that bring peace and happiness into my life on earth. I will drink of the nectar of God's love and be open to all the messages that bring divine understanding to my life.

At the Javits Convention Center in New York City, a friend and I attended Brian Weiss's workshop on, *"Many Lives, Many*

Masters: Experiencing Your Past Lives." At the workshop, we went through several intensive hypnotic regressions, which released my trepidations and worries about being in a meditative state.

I was able to undergo a deep meditative state that produced very positive results. For the very first time, I was able to read a person with accuracy. This was a monumental achievement that has become part of my life's path. Again, I give thanks for the experience that took place on Thanksgiving Day to open the way to knowing. My spiritual intentions are coming to light.

CHAPTER 6

Wisdom/Spirituality

The first book that captured my attention after my heart attack was, "How to Hear Your Angels" by Doreen Virtue. This spiritual guide provided me with a clear approach on how to converse with my angels and guides in the heavenly realm. I learned to disconnect from my self-image (ego) and focus on my spirituality through meditation. I can now clear my mind and reflect on many spiritual issues, such as taking the time to review my life events. I also think about who influenced me, for better or worse. Through divine guidance, I am able to communicate my needs, objectives and devotion to God in a well thought out manner.

On 1/11/12, I meditated using Doreen's CD, "The Best of Doreen Virtue/Past-Life Regression with the Angels." According to Wikipedia,

"Past life regression is a technique that uses hypnosis to recover what practitioners believe are memories of past lives or incarnations. Past Life regression is typically undertaken either in pursuit of a spiritual experience, or in a psychotherapeutic setting."[6]

Memories of past lives have had a profound effect on me. These experiences helped me become more conscious and capable as an individual to express my inner feelings to God and the universe. I am steadily progressing through different stages of consciousness. I am here because I choose to be here and the choice was the best thing that could happen to me.

While in a state of meditation, I became aware of three past lives. I was told by the angels, *"These two people were you in another life time and the third incident was you again as the same Dutchman on his death bed."*

During the first meditation, I regressed to a life as a wealthy 40 year old man in seventeenth century Holland. As I felt myself transition into the consciousness of this man, I looked down and saw that he was wearing a pair of Dutch wooden clogs. From the top of his shoes, I could see white stockings that came up just above his knees.

Then suddenly, I was outside looking at him from above. In his hands, he was carrying pieces of wood. In front of him, I saw a beautiful windmill. People were casually walking back and forth in front of the windmill. I looked up in the sky and saw it was blue as the ocean with mushroom silky clouds overhead.

While watching the Dutchman walking, I was amazed by the people around him. I couldn't help but notice how people responded to him. He was admired by the townspeople. He appeared to be affluent and a very powerful person in his community. He seemed enthusiastic about life and I sensed a peaceful presence around him. I knew in my heart that he was on his spiritual path. One could see that he was living a life of fulfillment and joy was his reward. Then suddenly, I was propelled in time and witness him dying.

The Dutchman was perhaps 70 or 80 years old. His face showed signs of serenity and love. A peaceful glow engulfed his very being. He seemed to be in harmony with the universe as well as tranquil in spirit. This was his final day as a bodily manifestation of a supernatural being here on Mother Earth.

The Dutchman was lying in a high wooden bed with silk lace covering his body. He was saying to himself, *"I am happy, I lived a good life and I am not afraid to die."* I could not see the rest of the room or tell if anyone was with him. In this life, he knew that death was a rebirth and a joyful occasion. I was watching his transition into spirit. I did feel my presence with him. I witnessed his last breath. He was at peace and I was at peace watching this fantastic experience.

What made me rejoice, in my meditation, was the fact that the Dutchman appeared to be a very wise man. Wisdom connotes strength, fortitude, and spirituality. These attributes were revealed to me in the way he walked, his body language, and how people looked at him with admiration and respect. Death was not his enemy but a peaceful journey home to be with his dearly beloved spirits guides, family and ancestors. He felt at peace with God.

In the same hypnosis session, I witnessed myself living in Paris, France in the 1890's. I was a 20 year old French woman named Emily. She was either a teacher or writer. In her hands, she was carrying books. Emily had on what look like a Peter Pan hat with several feathers on the side of the hat. The plumes were of different shades of green, brown and gold. Her dress was a very long green or brown ruffled outfit that went down to her ankles. On top of the dress, she wore a ruffled jacket made out of the same material.

She was walking with a young man. They were in deep conversation. I couldn't hear what was being said. However, I tried very hard to see who Emily was with. I said, *"can I see who she's with?"* Suddenly, a male face appeared in front of her body. Guess whose face it was? Yaw! My significant other in this incarnated life. I was so happy and I realized we had been together for many past lives. I wondered what the future incarnations would hold for us. Emily and Yaw were walking over a bridge. They were walking in the direction of the Eiffel Tower. What an extraordinary experience!

On January 15, 2012, I experienced an apparition while lying in my bed. A beautiful little girl of 3 or 4 walked through my bedroom and out the bedroom door through what I believe was a portal (between worlds going to the spirit world). She had long curly hair and was wearing a white multi-color flowered dress. I could only see her side profile and as she walked her back was facing me. She was holding a golden picture frame that was transparent. The see-through frame was half the size of her body but a little wider than she was. At the time, I wasn't aware of the symbolic meaning of this apparition.

On February 25, 2012, I attended a workshop, "Divine Connections with Love's Voice Circle of Love & Light," hosted by Bonny and Linda. The group meditation was clearly a powerful way to connect with the angels. During the meditation, I was overcome with feelings of love. Tears were flowing down my face. These were tears of inner peace and joy. I began telling my story to the spiritual group about my experiences on

Thanksgiving Day and the weeks and months that followed. I spoke about the little girl I had seen in my bedroom and the powerful light surrounding me with love after completing another meditation.

I was told by Marc Yale Brinkerhoff, (Clairvoyant, Clairaudient and Medium, a Mystic Artist, Soul Traveler and Animal Intuitive), *"This little girl was you. The golden frame represents, Your spiritual life's path on earth. The empty frame represents your openness to the spirit world and how you will be able to decide what directions in life you want to go to achieve your spiritual goals in this incarnated life as Carolyn."*

At this very same meeting, I mentioned my experience being in the presence of God or God's angelic guides or angels. After meditating in my bedroom one morning; a profound feeling of love overwhelmed and engulfed the entire room and me. Brilliant rays of sunlight encircled me and the room. It was as if I was taken possession of and was in a shield of divine love. The joy was so immense that I wept tears of blissful thanksgiving. I proclaimed out loud, *"Thank You God, Thank you God, Thank you God . . . ."* I had no negativity in my heart, only love. This love was illuminating from outside of me. Then this energy entered my body with a pure concentration of love.

Overwhelmed by this presence of love, I felt a deeper growing sense of understanding and love. I was moved from my very foundation. This must be how it feels living between lives with the angels and ancestors. While writing this and thinking about that very moment, it still brings tears of exultation and jubilation. For the rest of this life and for eternity, I will rejoice and celebrate the Creator's steadfast devotion to all things that have energy. God's divine energy manifests within everything. The Almighty's word was created from before time and will continue after time as we know time to be. Life will always be a continuum of God's powerful life force or energy.

While telling my story, I looked over and saw Marc crying. He said, *"I also had the same encounter."* Tears began to flow down my face again. Both of us had indescribable intense feelings during the experience. I now know that it may take a lifetime to comprehend the full experience and impact of our involvement with God's presence. In order to understand the full meaning of this event, I must stay on my path and live a life of devotion, love and joy. I will continue to attend spiritual workshops for encouragement and spiritual growth. Finding people who think like me is endearing and gives me peace of mind.

At a second encounter with Marc, I purchased a drawing of a mother bobcat (lynx) and two baby bobcats. Later on in my story I will reveal the spiritual connection between the two pictures. Cats have always played a very special role in my life especially after my heart attack.

At Bonny's workshop, I also met Alan DeValle; Alan is an Intuitive, Psychic Reader, and Musician. Alan gives workshops called, *"The Soul's Imperatives,"* a process that allows you to open up to your seven inner commands.

Alan is a spiritual brother who inspires me, provides guidance, and insights. He directs me on my path with inspiration, friendship, and love. His wisdom is insightful and truthful. He is a person I hold in a very special place in my heart.

At Bonny's workshop, Alan proclaimed, *"You were seeded from creation."* He also stated, *"You are a healer."* At first I didn't understand what he meant by seeded from creation. He explained, *"You may have been here at the very beginning of creation with God and the angels."* This statement left me speechless. That very statement shocked me and made me think of how many life times I may have lived?

Being *"seeded from creation,"* explains why some family members and friends say, I have always exhibited special insights or wisdom even as a child. I was around 5 or 6 years old, when a person rang my parent's door bell,

My mother opened the door; a well-dressed man asked my mother, *"Do you believe in God?"* My Mother replied, *"Yes"* and proceeded to talk to the man about many spiritual matters.

I was standing next to her listening to the whole conversation. I looked up at my mother with a beaming smile and said, *"He is a good man,"* and I walked away from the door. I felt I had to say this to my mother. This statement would change my life. My mother smiled with conviction, that next Sunday I attended Sunday school in a Presbyterian Church. As a teenager, I attended Presbyterian, Catholic and an all faith church. God is the creator of all people regardless of race, religion, or nationality. This is what I needed to learn from these different religious traditions. God is omnipotent and omnipresent. To me this means God is present in all religions, all races, all nationalities, and all things on Earth as well as below the Earth and above the Earth.

Brian L. Weiss, M.D. states,

"We change race, sex, religion, physical health or impairment, and nationality during our incarnations because we have to learn from all sides. We are rich, and we are poor, powerful and weak, Privileged and deprived. We learn by experiencing everything . . . Our bodies and relationships change, but the souls are the same. Your grandmother, for

instance, may reincarnate as your son. Same soul, different body, we have many soul mates, and we are always being reunited, either on the other side or back here, in the physical state."[7]

These transformations are part of human nature; living different reincarnated lives keeps us grounded spiritually. The lessons learned through multiple lifetimes enable us to let go of all fears from past lives and triumph over negativity in future lives. Living different lifestyles in each incarnation keeps us focused on our predetermined life paths. Our life paths give us opportunities to refine and perfect our soul lessons.

I have a few memories of other past lives. One was a glimpse of me as a male Christian minister named Frank. This past life regression took me to the early 1900's in the mid-west. Frank was wearing a long black coat with white lace shirt and a black thin rope tie around his neck. The minister had on brown cowboy boots. He was preaching a fire and brimstone sermon to 20 or 30 church members. With arms thrusting, he was telling the church members that there is such a place as hell, where the wicked shall be tormented forever.

I was listening to the sermon; however, with tears in my eyes, I started yelling, *"No, it's not true. I no longer believe in fire and brimstone in my present life."* I suddenly departed from the past life experience. One thing that I have come to realize is that we do the best we can with what we understand. We must not judge others or ourselves. Since I am sure that I have made many mistakes in previous lives, I have learned those lessons and will move on to learn more inspired lessons.

Another memory of a past life was of a Senegalese boy fifteen or sixteen years old. He was kneeling in the middle of an open field of grass looking in all directions. He had on a body wrap. The Senegalese boy had sharp features with a beautiful black hue. There were mountains in the back ground. There was no one in sight. I was looking at the boy's surroundings and trying to locate the area he lived in. I received only minimal information during this past life experience. There was serenity, natural harmony in the Senegalese boy that was totally absent in Minister Frank.

As this vision closed and then opened again I saw an angel. This figure started out as light energy. Then this brilliant light energy took on form of a male or female angel with wings. There were no facial details at all. I could only see this angel from a distance. Then the angel disappeared from my view. After this encounter, I have seen other angels in a variety of silhouettes, shades, and sizes. I have felt their energy presence around me.

These were beautiful experiences that inspired me to stay on my life's course. All of these experiences are valuable tools for me to connect to the Source, the angels, my ancestors and the universe. I am able to revisit some of my past lives and witness many beautiful things in this life. This is a spiritual gift we have as earthly spiritual beings. To understand my experiences and life's purpose I did my Soul's Imperatives.

CHAPTER 7

My Soul's Imperatives: Spiritual Journey

Since my NDE, people, books, and spiritual experiences have opened the door wider for me to express my spirituality. The Soul's Imperatives is one tool I used to manifest and examine my life's purpose.

On March 16, 2012, Alan DeValle performed a *Soul's Imperative Seven Points,"* insights and application pertaining to my spiritual journey. A week later, I performed on myself a second Soul's Imperatives.

Carolyn Reid, I am here to:

- Understand—By writing "Stay or Go" (my journey) I will obtain inner wisdom or forgotten knowledge from above.
- My role is to help—To transform my life and help others in their journey.
- Deliver—Distribute my book and jewelry as my creative gift to the universe.
- Love—I need to send out to the universe unconditional peace and love.
- Explore—I will investigate all aspects of Spirituality to ensure inner balance.
- Move—I can reclaim my spiritual path with the qualities of a shaman or priest.
- Act—All my actions and thoughts be guided by God, angels and my ancestors.

Booster Imperatives—These are additional soul intentions to manifest and develop positive life choices in my incarnation on Mother Earth:

- * Create—Write a spiritual book and design unique jewelry.
- * Expand—Increase my spiritual work.
- * Produce—Mediate on the book becoming a movie someday.
- * Travel—London, Brazil and the world—2013-2016

I am consciously affirming my soul's imperative to become more divinely inspired, more energetically charged, and more liberated in thought and action. As my consciousness becomes more developed and logical, I will gain greater access to my higher self and perhaps obtain a higher level of spirituality. My spirituality, in this life time, will help me in my next incarnated life and in living between lives with God and the angels.

On March 25, 2012, I tuned in to Dr. Wayne Dyer on Oprah Winfrey Network (OWN) for Super Soul Sunday. What a unique and inspiring soulful episode. Oprah Winfrey orchestrated a mindful, informative and reaffirming platform for Dr. Dyer's commentary on "Wishes Fulfilled: Mastering the Art of Manifesting."

According to Dr. Dyer,

> *"In order to know something spiritually, you must experience it, there is no other way-You cannot simply think your way to a new awareness. You must experience it, and the only vehicles you have for directly experiencing a new and higher vision for yourself are your feelings. Your feelings are where you live. If you have been able to assume the feeling within your heart and genuinely feel the love that this activity brings to you, you, as Neville states: will be in a place where your wish must be realized-such is the power of your feelings."*[8]

One's feelings or thoughts reflect the essence of creation itself. Feelings are the perfect thread between this world and living between worlds. Our beliefs are the emotional state or reaction to the oneness of The Divine. Feeling connected to the spirit world, enforces one's ability to manifest all that one desires. Through meditation all these things are possible. God's divinity is the life force (vibrational energy) that flows through eternity.

On April 20, 2012, a friend and I attended Angel Certification Program (ACP) with Charles Virtue and Tina Daly. This workshop was located at the Hyatt Hotel, in Morristown, New Jersey. The ACP class was one of the most joyful, informative, and life changing experiences thus far. This conference opened the door for me to use my intuitive skills to read other people. This spiritual conference would eliminate my fears of performing a Life-Purpose reading. The main purpose of this class was to teach self-healing and skill building.

In self-healing, I learned to release blocks, fears, and unwanted painful feelings. I also learned how to let go of past life fears. I was able to listen to the voices of the angels. This tool opened the door to become divinely guided.

Skill building allowed me to learn how to perform angel readings using Doreen Virtue's, Life Purpose Oracle cards. I was spiritually awakened by the angels of light. I learned to bypass my ego and let the angels work through me and for me. All of us have this ability to read people. We are the instrument by which the angels provide the information to counsel clients with love, peace, and compassion.

On the second day of the conference, during the workshop an amazing enlightenment took place. The night before, I was meditating. My body was traveling down a country road going at a fast speed. I could see, on both sides of the road, beautiful trees. The car was moving, but I was moving not in the car but over the car. I saw beautiful houses and spacious landscapes. It was a very tranquil and sunlit day.

The next day, we performed a reading on each other. One student asked, *"Can I do a reading on you?"* I replied, *"Yes, you can."* During her reading, she began by saying, *"I see you driving down a country road." There were many lamp posts on each side of the road."* I asked, *"What does this all mean, because I had the same vision last night?"* The student called over to Tina and said, *"I see Carolyn driving down a country road and on each side of the road there were many lamp posts. What was the meaning of my reading?"* The student asked. Tina replied, *"Were the lamp posts on or off?"* The reader replied, *"all the lamp posts were on."* Tina responded, *"The lamp posts indicate that Carolyn is on her path."* I left that student and went in the back of the room and found another student name Janet.

"Hi Janet, Would you like to do a reading on me?" "Yes," Janet replied, *"for some reason I really wanted to do a reading on you."* So Janet began, by saying, *"I see you going down a country road with the lamp posts on. Archangel Michael, (powerful Guardian and Healer) lighting your way. He is connected to Archangel Root who protects you from evil and brings good luck in health and family matters."* I started to cry because this information was so powerful. I was amazed and astonished by the other student's reading. I was destined to be at this conference.

Janet was excited and extremely happy that we both were able to read each other with clarity and accuracy. We both began to cry because we both knew at the same time we were supposed to meet and exchange these messages. We bonded spiritually together that day. We continue to talk to each other when needed or just to say hello.

The energy at the conference was awesome and inspiring. We learned to work with the major archangels and ascended masters to connect with our ancestors. We also practiced new psychic and healing skills on each other to build our confidence as healers and readers.

On April 25, 2012, Janet emailed me, "I *hope you are still in the beautiful vibration of the angels! I absolutely needed to write; as I am getting some messages that you're meant to hear and see for yourself! It appears as though you will understand when you see them!*" Attached to Janet's email was a picture of a dragon and an owl. I did some research.

According to D.J. Conway, many Old and New World cultures acknowledge the dragon symbol. *"In spiritual definitions: The dragon represents the supernatural, infinity itself, and the spiritual powers of change and transformation. It is a fierce protector..."*[9]

Another friend told me that these spirit dragons are our way of letting go of our deepest fears that will block our spirituality. Many cultures use the dragon totems to free themselves from negative energy. Cole, R.J. states in his website,

> "The *most common message a Dragon totem carries to us is a need for strength, courage, and fortitude. Dragons are also messengers of balance, and magic—encouraging us to tap into our psychic nature and see the world through the eyes of mystery and wonder. More specifically, Dragons are the embodiment of primordial power—The ultimate ruler of all the elements, this is because the Dragon is the made of all the elements: Fire, Water, Earth, and Wind."*[10]

Janet also mentioned the owl as one of my totem animals. The owl suggests wisdom, strength, and clairvoyance. According to The Owl Totem, owls have the following qualities:

"Powerful magic, good omens, prophecy, astral travel, power to see the un-seen, all seeing knowledge, great *wisdom, good luck, power of the moon and night, insight giving and receiving . . . The Owl animal totem is a strong* spirit indeed *and its magical properties are one of the most influential of all animal totems. Strength, virtue, and religious beliefs can be integrated into the spirit of the possessor of this magical pearl and the Owl totem."*[11]

Janet had acknowledged in her reading of me, that in one of my past lives I may have been a Native American from the Cherokee Nation. When she returned home she had a strong desire to email me this information. I responded with a call to her. I told Janet: *"Thanks for thinking about me. I have read all the information you sent. I am in the process of knowing. This information will help me on my spiritual journey. In time I pray that all this powerful wisdom will be a part of my spiritual being here on Mother Earth."*

CHAPTER 8

Mystical Retreat

Because of my NDE, the weekend of September, 28, 2012, I attended Rev. Bonny and Rev. Linda's retreat: "Awaken Your True Identity: Developing Inner Awareness." This magnificent mystical gathering was at the Spiritual Center nestled in the beautiful hills of Windsor, New York. This powerful sacred site is run by spiritual sisters who by their commitment, charitable natures, and loving hearts open their doors for spiritual events. Bonny and Linda were the overseers of this event. Together, they enriched my understanding and awareness of a greater self. This monumental spiritual haven had become for me, an electrifying and moving experience that I would never forget.

Aisha, and two friends and I arrived at the Spiritual Center at approximately 4:30 pm. There were twelve attendees at the retreat. We were introduced to five nuns of The Joseph of Carondelet's order. We were embraced by their loving spirit. They truly cared about all of us spiritually, and provided us with great food to nourish our bodies. After we finished eating, we went into a second room to meditate with Bonny and Linda.

While meditating, I felt my spirit rising from my body. This spirit movement was a new phenomenon. I can't wait until I am able to leave my body one day and explore the universe. Spirit can achieve anything. Spirit is my direct link to my higher thoughts and feelings. These thoughts and feelings give me the ability to create and manifest more abundance in my life.

My thoughts and feelings are my teaching tools for my spiritual journey. I experience what I need to in order to achieve balance in my life. Through my thoughts and feelings I have direct contact to The Source by which all things are governed by His/Hers perfect laws. I look to God for all my needs. God is all-powerful all-knowing, and fully present in every moment of my life.

After Friday night's session I went to bed. While lying in my bed with my eyes closed, I started seeing faces, that were light in color, one after the other. Were these more past lives? I have no idea to whom these faces belonged. Maybe someday I will remember who they are in relation to me.

Saturday morning breakfast was available from 7:30-8:30 am. We selected different tables at each meal time in order for everyone to become acquainted. I found the group very diverse with different and unique talents and interests. A sense of compassion and caring permeated the whole retreat. A feeling of gratitude, love, and spiritual insight was about to be rediscovered. I was immediately at ease in this community of kindred spirits and we were about to experience a magnificent journey into the spirit world. There was a synchronicity among the members of our group that made it easy to explore our spirituality together.

After we ate breakfast, the group participated in several sessions. Before the first session started, Bonnie said: *"Please select a chair and take a look at the material that was left for you to read."* One of the items on my chair was a picture frame that was facing down. I couldn't see what was in it. When I picked up my frame, I saw a picture of a bobcat (lynx). I believe there are no coincidences in life. Remember, I previously purchased from Marc, a picture of three bobcats many months prior to attending this retreat.

The bobcat represents hidden, unseen, but unforgotten secrets or spiritual truths. The bobcat also symbolizes balance in the universe. They possess an expansive consciousness and keen insight into the spirit world. They are trustworthy and loyal guides even as they appear fearsome. The bobcat conveys the ability to see and uncover lies. As spiritual teachers of conscious, knowing beings bobcats possess awareness and insight on our thoughts, dreams, and visions.

In thinking about bobcats, I can't help but reflect on Heidi and Chloe, the cats in my life. They became my bodyguards and babysitters while I was at Aisha's house recuperating from my surgery. The cats would curl up next to me for hours on end. They are so spiritual, loving, and devoted. If I moved one muscle, they were up and ready to investigate. They sensed I was sick or knew that something was different about my behavior. They tried in every way to keep me lying down. At different times, one or the other cat, would sit on my chest and stay there for long periods of time. Both cats helped me in my healing process. How wonderful is God's love for us, to have given us such a gift as profound and gorgeous as animals to love. I am very thankful for realizing the role animals play on earth and in the heavens.

I became connected to the cats. We bonded together as one. At times, I felt that the cats understood my health situation better than I did. They knew I needed rest and consoling. I felt the cats had healing powers. In their presence, I felt more relaxed and calm. They helped to facilitate my healing process. I am very grateful and thankful to God for giving me living creatures to watch over me in times of need.

During another session, on Psychometrics or Psychometry (focusing on a picture and getting impressions from the spirit world) the group was asked to bring a photo of a loved one, someone in spirit or still here on Mother Earth. We were also asked, to bring an object that belonged to a loved one. We were then told to select items and photos that had historical significance in our lives.

At the workshop, we were sitting in a horseshoe semi-circle waiting for instructions from Bonny and Linda. The group placed all the items on the floor and each of us selected a picture of a person of whom we had no knowledge. I selected a picture of a young girl. This girl was a relative of Bonny and Linda's. While holding the picture, I closed my eyes and immediately relaxed and listened to my thoughts, I focused on the whole picture, and I saw an unborn fetus in an amniotic sac. The sac was transparent. I could see that the baby was almost full term. I told the group what I had seen. Bonny looked at Linda and said, *"Carolyn went all the way back to the womb."* The other students took turns describing what they encountered from their experience. They all had extraordinary stories to tell about the items they picked.

The next item I picked up was a cloth key chain. I closed my eyes and held the key chain for about five minutes. While holding the key chain I cleared my thoughts and asked for guidance from the angels. The object became extremely warm, almost hot, to the touch. I said out loud, *"The person this key chain belongs to felt very safe and secure in this house. This house was a safe haven for you. A lot of love was in this house."* Two classmates acknowledge that the key chain belonged to them with tears in their eyes. They both indicated that, indeed, the house was a safe haven for them as children.

The most life changing experience I had at the retreat was while sitting in a dark room with a photo of Mother Meera. Mother Meera, "an incarnation of the Divine Mother was born in South India.... In 2006 Mother resumed touring the world to give Darshan. The Darshan blessing, *"A bestowal of Love, Light and Grace is offered to all, free of charge, independent of spiritual beliefs or affiliations. The blessing has been said to remove obstacles to spiritual fulfillment and to answer the heart's prayer."*[12]

In a dark and serene room, I sat in a chair with my head bowed down. With both hands on my knees, I meditated for a few minutes. When I looked up at Mother Meera's picture I felt the wisdom and joy etched in her face. At first I witness a soft light on the left side of her face. Then a fresh breeze seemed to flow across her face. Before my very eyes she came alive. I could see slight movement in her face. Her eyes were looking straight into mine. I felt her powerful love. Then her whole face came alive. I felt peaceful. I heard these words: *"You will receive what you are asking for."*

I got up from the chair and went into the dining room where Bonny, Linda and a friend were sitting and vocalized in a loud tone, *"Wow, I can't believe what just . . ."* Bonny quieted me. I had forgotten that others were in the same dark room next to the kitchen taking turns to be in the presence of Mother Meera. I went into another area and took a moment to reflect on the healing and transformation I received on 11/24/11. I felt a sense of oneness with all life and began to contemplate the relationship of Mother Meera's silence to my spiritual journey.

Mother Meera states,

> *"I do not speak but my force changes people completely. The power of the Divine works in the silence and will change things according to your aim and what you ask for. Sometimes I can give immediately what you have requested. Sometimes it takes time."*[13]

The Divine Mother is an example of love at its highest spiritual level and we are blessed to have such a person living amongst us. She is an inspiration to all. She invokes divine favor upon all who happen to meet her in person or those who view her avatar. She opens a path to healing, protection and transformation. I felt blessed by my experience of her brilliant light and love.

Another session began. Chosen as the first to participate, I sat in front of the group, in the dark, with a white candle in front of me. I started feeling myself transforming from this incarnated life into past lives. I felt an energy force coming from the bottom of my neck up to the top of my head. I could feel the structure of my face shifting. This facial shifting brought memories of past lives I had experienced while meditating. As I felt my face transforming I recognized each past life. I began to introduce them to the group. I could hear people in the group saying, *"Look at her face, she's"* I said, *"Am I a male with long curly brown hair?"* Someone said, *"Yes"* I then said, *"That was me as Frank, the male Christian Minister. I was preaching a sermon on fire and brimstone. I was saying to the Minister while he was giving his sermon, I no longer believed in fire and brimstone in my present life. There is no hell."*

Then my face changed again, I appeared as a female, Buddhist Monk and then as a Native American. Every time I changed I could feel the transformation. I appeared as the forty year old Dutchman who lived in the Netherlands. I was so happy that the group had a chance to see him. They all were astonished. For some reason he stands out the most to me because I had the chance to see him twice in my past life regressions. The spiritual group had a chance to see him and how he looked. The group was surprised to witness the change of race, sex and religion that took place as I was sitting in the dark with my eyes closed. I heard Aisha say, *"She's looking at me, she's looking at me."* Everyone became very quiet in the room. The rest of the group started to take turns viewing their own different incarnations.

Saturday night we met and placed our names in a dish in order to select which one's dearly departed loved ones would come through. A group member picked Vera's name out of the disk to meditate on. We began to meditate. While I was meditating, a voice said, *"Tell her I love her."* First the voice was soft. But I didn't want to say anything so the voice became louder. Still I didn't want to say anything because I wasn't sure who was speaking to me. The voice became even louder, *"Tell her I love her."* I said, *"O.K."* I finally blurted out. Your Mother said, *"She loves you, Vera."* This surprised Vera who had not seen or heard from her mother in 20 years. Vera said, *"Carolyn guess what my mother's name is?"* I said: *"Please tell me."* She said *"Carol."* I said," *Vera most people call me Carol."* We hugged each other. No more words were said that night between us.

The next morning we meditated on manifesting our dreams. Vera's Mother came through again. *"Tell her I love her."* I couldn't meditate because Vera's mother kept saying, *"Tell her I love her."* So finally I said, your mother said, *"She loves you."* This was the second time in this incarnated life I was able to receive messages from beyond, from someone's loved one. Vera acknowledged the message.

On another occasion at the Spiritual Center, we engaged in spiritual art. We would choose a person and create a spiritual drawing. We picked the color paper we wanted to use for the activity. Then with closes eyes we picked colored crayons and drew with them. The person who chose me picked up my beloved brother Alvin's spirit vibrations. I know this was his spirit because she was right handed but after she finish the picture she said, *"Carolyn I couldn't use my right hand to draw."* I told her, *"My brother was left handed."* Second, she drew DNA on the paper. My brother wanted me to know that he knew I had just taken a DNA test the week before this retreat. I was delighted to encounter my brother for the first time since his passing. I wondered why I had not been able to connect with him before. We were extremely close. I realize now he is watching over me as he did when we were growing up together. There is a circle of life and light that flows through all of us and connects us to each other and to our Creator.

CHAPTER 9

The Beginning

My story is just beginning. I was given a second chance at life. My NDE was a profound physical, emotional, and spiritual experience that was life-changing. As a result, I now live a life of gratitude and faith.

I believe I've received a glimpse of how the angels assist us here on Mother Earth, as well as a chance to learn from my past lives. I now know that everything I have done in this life and other lifetimes has been part of a plan my soul contracted before each birth. Included in my plan was every adversity, suffering, and heartache, including the events of 11/24/11, as well as every moment of joy and bliss in this lifetime.

Of primary importance to the shifting of my consciousness was my realization that it was fear and anxiety that had been interfering with my destiny. I now intimately understand the message of all great spiritual teachings. Love, compassion, and everlasting life are God's gift to all of us. Spirit is the Spirit in me and the Spirit is all that ever was and will be.

My search for God opened my heart and heightened my creativity. My business is growing and transforming into a high end collection of fine jewelry. My website is in production. Love, peace, and joy come to fruition daily as I continue to meet and learn from others in my work and spiritual endeavors.

The rich awareness that now illuminates my journey is filled with a sense of God's love and wisdom guiding all I do, all I am. I proceed with confidence that life does not end but is an ongoing part of the evolution of the spirit. As I continue to search for spiritual truths I embrace this blissful sense of oneness with God and send love into the universe. I humbly offer my story to encourage others on their journey.

CHAPTER 10

8 Readings from The Crystal Tarot: Reflections and Reaffirmations

Tarot cards are a valuable tool to help me connect to the Source, the angels, my ancestors, and the wisdom of the subconscious. At the end of this book, I present my interpretation of Phillip Permutt's Crystal Tarot cards in the hope of establishing balance, clarity, and confirmation of my path.

For each reading, I selected three cards to represent the past, present, and the future. "Drop cards" are any cards that fall from the deck while shuffling. I have included them as having special significance in my readings.

*The "past" card represents what has occurred in my past that directly affects my question.

*The "present" card represents the energy or influences currently surrounding my question.

*The "future" card represents the likely outcome of my question.

Transformation

Before selecting three cards, I meditated on the miracle that occurred on 11/24/11 which transformed my preconceptions of God, life, and the spirit world around me and opened me to a new spiritual perspective.

The Reading #1: The transformation on Thanksgiving Day broke the spell of past beliefs and opened me up to new found spiritual viewpoints.

<u>Past</u>-Interpretation

Ace Swords—You had a spiritual breakthrough on 11/24/11. A positive transformation happened to make way for your spiritual awakening. View the world with objectivity. Compassion, tolerance, and understanding will lead you to your life purpose. With the help of Archangel Gabriel you will be able to write your story. Creative opportunities are coming your way. The sword cuts deep into you spiritual core bringing balance, flexibility and new beginnings.

<u>Present</u>-Interpretation

King Pentacles—You can create your dreams and bring them to fruition. You are in control of your destiny. Reap your rewards. You are a divine being experiencing life and learning from your guides. You are in control of your destiny. Money may come your way but knowledge is more important to you. You have the power to flourish and to conquer your fears.

<u>Future</u>-Interpretation

Queen Pentacles-Mother Nature surrounds you with love and keeps you firmly grounded. The shield protects you and prohibits blocks that are in your way. You are a compassionate person. The four circle flowers on each corner represent your enlightenment, the way, or the door to the afterlife.

<u>Drop Card</u>-Interpretation-These are cards that dropped out of my hands while I was scuffling the desk.

The Star XV11-You are free. You are in harmony with the universe. Water is the sign that you are flowing through life peacefully. You are open to all possibilities. You are discerning, empowered and loved.

The Denial

My attempt to deny my illness, that eventful Thanksgiving Day was the beginning of my awakening to forgotten truths and self-knowledge. I truly remembered experiencing enormous fear that morning. I understand now that this fear was not because I thought I was dying but because I had not fulfilled my dreams and spiritual purpose in this life. This awakening was facilitated by my decision to stay. I needed my earthly life to be restored. I performed the next reading to meditate upon my denial of illness on 11/24/11.

The Reading #2: Could I have foreseen this ahead of time?

<u>Past</u>-Interpretation
Nine Cups-Your cups are running over rejoice and be happy. Life is not always this fulfilling. You need to store up your money or spiritual gifts for another day.

<u>Present</u>-Interpretation
Eight Cups-The white stars suggests that you are looking for inspiration. The crystals in the cups are not smooth which means you need to go in a different direction in life. Do not deny your health. Keep a watchful eye on your food intake.

<u>Future</u>-Interpretation
The High Priest—Connection to the spirit world. The High Priest is the mirror to the universe. You are wise, demonstrate powerful healing powers, and your feet are firmly planted on the ground. Meaning you are completely open spiritually.

The Divine Intervention/Crucial Moment in Time

The third reading is based on the divine intervention I received on my way to the hospital, at the hospital, and during the operation. The angels were watching over me and guiding me to my destiny. This was a crucial moment in time for a very important decision I had to make. I asked the cards for clarification on the events of that day.

The Reading #3: God's intervention at a crucial moment in time.

Past-Interpretation

Ten Pentacles-You are deeply rooted in your spiritual development. Everything is coming together. You are powerful, confident and secure. Let the positive energy guide your decisions that will keep you firmly on your path.

Present-Interpretation

Nine Pentacles-You are on your path however, try not to doubt your intuition. Stay on your path even when fears try to creep into your mind. Enjoy what you have already planted spiritually and be happy. Forgive yourself and others.

Future-Interpretation

Eight Pentacles-You are still on your path but you have a lot of work to be done. Do not stop writing. Be creative, your book is valuable and worthwhile. Stay on track, success is around the corner. God has given you all the tools you will need to complete your mission.

1st. <u>Drop Card</u>-Interpretation

The World XXI-The raft represents completion. Your cycle has ended. A new beginning has started. Meditate and envision that this new path will lead you to a higher level of consciousness. Success is coming your way.

2nd. <u>Drop Card</u>-Interpretation

Judgment XX-You are calling on your inner child. The child in you will lead the way and clear your path. The angels are with you and will help you find your way. Ask for guidance and you will receive all the counseling you need. The angel's guidance will enhance your ability to handle changes. You will feel comfortable with your choices.

The Awakening

I clearly comprehend that in order to awaken to one's divine self-one must surrender to love, faith, and tolerance. I must willingly sacrifice myself; have patience and gratitude for all things spiritual. But most of all, I must have complete devotion to God. With devotion to God, I can demonstrate my love to others and help to generate peace here on Mother Earth. Having prearranged my life's events before birth, I understand now that there is no need for fear as I embrace this authentic mystical experience. Spiritual transformations have taken place at different stages in my life to help me connect to my higher self. I consulted the cards to gain insight about my spiritual awakening. These spiritual transformations take place at different stages in my life to help me to connect to my higher self. I consulted the cards to gain insight about my spiritual awakenings.

The Reading #4: Spiritual truths.

<u>Past</u>-Interpretation

King Cups—You are sitting on the throne and your life is about to change. You seem anxious. The waves behind you signify turbulence in your life. Focus on what direction in life you want to take. A transformation is about to take place.

<u>Present</u>-Interpretation

Three Cups-Your cup is running over. Good times are coming. Be happy, contented and flexible. The waves represent new friends or new ideas. These friends or ideas will help you on your journey. Have fun! You have worked hard now you need to celebrate.

Future-Interpretation

Five Wands-You are still on your path. But, be aware of obstacles in front of you. These things that obstruct progress are only temporary. Stay the course. Fire represents danger. You will encounter pit falls. Stand your ground. Be mindful of incidents that will take you off your course.

Daughter's Devotion

My gratitude will never waver because God and the angels let me stay with my wonderful daughter. I am blessed. I couldn't be more grateful to be Aisha's mother. I have 33 years with her. The best 33 years of my life and counting. The flow of the divine energy between us will last for eternity. I meditated on my relationship with my daughter in the following reading.

The Reading #5: Daughter's Love.

Past-Interpretation

Four Swords—You are cutting through old ideas. But you need to keep the ideas that will benefit, ground, and heal you. The universe is on your side. The cosmos is declaring—it is time to rejuvenate and give yourself new energy to continue on your course. Your daughter's love is the most important thing in your life. She feels the same way too.

Present-Interpretation

The High Priestess—Your resilience bears fruit. You are steadfast in obtaining some of your goals which were put in place before you came to earth. God and the angels are keeping you on your predestination here on earth. The light encircles your entire body giving you divine protection. The new moon sets the stage for new beginnings. You will complete or almost complete many of your life purposes here on earth. Your heart is filled with joy.

Future Interpretation

111 The Empress-You are in control of your destiny. Your greatest joy in life was giving birth to your daughter. She has

changed your life. You have become more creative, productive, and centered. She brings out the childlike qualities in you. The road is open to you. Keep building on your spirituality. You see the beauty of nature all around you. You are very optimistic about your future.

<u>Spiritual Animals</u>

Animals are spiritual beings. They are analytical, adaptable, and exceedingly clever spirits. They are consistent, non-judgmental, and their love is unconditional. Animals teach us to be compassionate, loving, and respectful of other spirit beings. They convey to us qualities we need or that are lacking in our lives. These wonderful beings regardless of species and location, teach us how to connect to all things on earth and in the universe. I consulted the cards about the meaning of animals in my life.

The Reading #6: Animals provide love and in turn, they became our allies in life.

<u>Past</u>—Interpretation
Queen Wands—The animal's world is very much a part of our lives. They are not afraid of mankind's spirit. They see you as you truly are. The Queen sits on her throne with authority, wisdom and control. This can be you in the future. Take charge!

<u>Present</u>—Interpretation
Knight Wands-You are on a journey or spiritual quest. You are prepared to take on life. The horse is signaling you to wait and take your time. You will need some help. Do not rush into anything. Use caution and avoid danger.

<u>Future</u>—Interpretation
Queen Cups—Like your animal guides, you have stored up your treasures. You are free to be a healer, writer, or a reader. You are open to others and in harmony with yourself. You can use all of your gifts to help and influence others.

Meditation/ Inspiration

Meditation opens the mind of humankind to receive inspiration. Simply open your heart and receive the sacred gift of forgotten truths that dwell in all of us. Meditation is a direct path to the Creator. It calms, relaxes, and alternately takes you to wisdom, truths, and finally enlightenment. The following reading was an open meditation.

The Reading #7: Daily meditation will open doors that you never thought existed.

Past—Interpretation

Seven Cups-Opportunities are still coming your way. Choose these prospects wisely. Don't let time be your enemy. Use time as a tool to accomplish your goals. Stay focused, organize your thoughts. Things will fall into place soon. Keep communicating with the angels. They will guide you all the way.

Present-Interpretation

Queen Wands-Sit back and enjoy the journey. You are in the mist of completing all that you need to finish, and start on a new path. Enjoy the ride. You are in control of your destiny. You are focused; trust in yourself. Your spirit's guides are keeping you balanced.

Future-Interpretation

Ace Wands-Fire evokes fear, doubt, and failure to take on new opportunities. You can overcome your fears by not letting emotional blocks enter your consciousness. Meditate, Meditate . . . . Do not ponder on past life events.

1st. Drop Cards-Interpretation

Page Pentacles—Money is a tool. Use your money wisely. Invest in your future. Have your jewelry website designed. Finish writing your book. You have the money and time to accomplish all your dreams. Have faith!

2nd. Drop Card-Interpretation—The Magician-Everything is on the table. The magician can do anything. This is your time to create and manifests all your hearts desires. Use this time wisely. Everything is coming together at work, home, and in your friendships. Use your creativity to its fullest potential. Have fun!

3rd. Drop Card-Interpretation Eight Wands—Fire—Do not let opportunities pass you by. Wands can point you in the right direction. Use stumbling blocks in your life to direct you and keep you focused. Listen to people who came before you.

Wisdom/Spirituality

My richer sense of self has transformed my way of thinking of myself as an artist and spiritual person; I have encompassed a greater sense of who I am and who I can be. Everything on earth affects everything in the universe. Be in harmony with yourself, family, and friends. Send your love out into the universe to light the way. The last reading was an open general reading on the subject of wisdom and spirituality in my life.

Past Interpretation

Two Swords-Analyze and dissect all your options. Be careful not to make the wrong decisions. Let your wisdom guide you through your journey. Trust in what you have experienced. Be hands on with all that you see and do.

The Reading #8: Spiritual truths and life lessons.

Present—Interpretation

The Empress-Your heart is open to all that is spiritual. You are a positive person. You are happy and confident. Nature is what makes you the happiest. It seems you have an abundance of love, creativity and peace in your life. Work hard and enjoy the benefits. Take time out for yourself so you can smell the roses.

Future Interpretation

Three Pentacles—Pay off your bills and steer clear of negative emotions. Keep love, peace, and joy in your day to day activities. Don't let anger uproot your positive energy. A shield of love will keep you focused on your task ahead.

1st. Drop Card

<u>Future</u>—Interpretation

Eight Pentacles-You are well planted in your pursuits of spiritual development. These spiritual pursuits will help you succeed and conquer your fears. You are on the right track. Continue to write, cultivate your business and importantly, stay on your path. Do not abandon your dreams.

References

1. The Holy Bible: King James Version. Harrisonburg, VA. : A Meridian Book, 1974.
2. Ibid., 191
3. Newton, M. (2011). Memories of the afterlife. (5 ed., p. 77). Woodbury, Minnesota: Llewellyn Publication.
4. Virtue, D. (2011). The healing miracles of Archangel Raphael. (1st ed., p. xiv). Carlsbad, California: Hay House, INC.
5. McGough, R. A. (2013). Historical archive of the bible wheel site. Retrieved from http://www.biblewheel.com/Topics/seven.php.
6. Wikipedia. (2012). Past life regression. Retrieved, 2012, from http://wikipedia.org/wiki/Past_life_ regression.
7. Weiss M.D., B. L. (2008). Many lives, many masters. (p. 220). New York, NY: Simon& Schuster.

8. Dyer, W. (2012). Wishes fulfilled. (1st ed., p. 101). Carlsbad, California: Hay House, INC.

9. Conway, D. J. (2003). Animal magick: the art of recognizing & working with familiars. Woodbury, MN: Llewellyn Publications.

10. Cole, R. J. (2009). A guide to dream interpretation. Retrieved from Dragon's in dreams? A Guidebook to Dream interpretation: Dream meanings for inner discovery. http://thedreamingswizard.com/-dragon-symbol 236.html.

11. The owl totem. (2013, May 22). Retrieved from Owl Totem Spiritual Wisdom Spiritual Meditation Spiritual Life Styles Spiritual. http://www.manizone.co.uk/the-owl-totem--a-6.html.

12. The silent darshan of mother meera. (n.d.). Retrieved from http://mothermeerafoundationusa/darshan.html.

13. Library of quotes from mother. (n.d.). Retrieved from http://mothermeeracorvallis.com/Main/corvallis/cor-quotes.jsp.

14. Permutt, P. (2010). The crystal tarot. New York: CICO Books.

Bibliography

Alexander, E. (2012). *Proof of heaven.* [United States]: Simon and Schuster Audio.

Anderson, G., & Barone, A. (1999). *Lessons from the light: Extraordinary messages of comfort and hope from the other side.* New York: Putnam.

Betty, S. (2011). The afterlife unveiled what the dead are telling us about their world.O-books.

Choquette, S. (2006). *Ask your guides: Connecting to your divine support system.* Carlsbad, Calif.: Hay House.

Dyer, W. W. (2007). *Change your thoughts, change your life: Living the wisdom of the tao.* Carlsbad, Calif.: Hay House.

Dyer, W. W. (2009). *Excuses begone!: How to change lifelong, self-defeating thinking habits.* Carlsbad, Calif.: Hay House.

Dyer, W. W. (2012). *Wishes fulfilled: Mastering the art of manifesting.* Carlsbad, Calif.: Hay House.

Farmer, S. (2007). *Messages from your animal spirit guide [a meditation journey].* [Carlsbad, CA]: Hay House Audio.

Hay, L. L., & Hay House Audio. (2004). *I can do it.* [Carlsbad, CA]: Hay House Audio.

Hay, L. L., & Richardson, C. (2011). *You can create an exceptional life.* Carlsbad, Calif.: Hay House.

Johnston, S. D. (2012). *Invoking the archangels: A nine-step process to heal your body, mind, and soul.* San Antonio, Tex.; London: Hierophant; Deep [distributor].

Kempton, S. (2011). *Beginning meditation [enjoying your own deepest experience].* Boulder, CO: Sounds True.

Life purpose oracle cards. (2011). Hay House Inc.

Martin, J., Bashe, P. R., & Anderson, G. (1988). *We don't die: George anderson's conversations with the other side.* New York: G.P. Putnam's Sons.

Martin, nickolas, edd, & martin, linda M . . . mhd. ego and spirituality the consciousness of egospiritualism. (2012). Balboa Pr.

Mehl-Madrona, L., & Sounds True (Firm). (2011). *The spirit of healing stories, wisdom, and practices from native america.* Boulder, CO: Sounds True.

Moorjani, A., (2012). *Dying to be me: My journey from cancer, to near death, to true healing.* Carlsbad, Calif.: Hay House.

Newton, M. (1994). *Journey of souls: Case studies of life between lives.* St. Paul, Minn.: Llewellyn.

Newton, M. (2000). *Destiny of souls: New case studies of life between lives.* St. Paul, Minn.: Llewellyn Publications.

Newton, M., & Michael Newton Institute. (2009). *Memories of the afterlife: Life between lives stories of personal transformation.* Woodbury, Minn.: Llewellyn Publications.

Permutt, P. (2010). *The crystal tarot.* Cico Books.

Solnado, A. (2011). *The book of light: Ask and heaven will answer.* New York: Atria Paperback.

Three Initiates, Deslippe, P., & Atkinson, W. W., (2011). *The kybalion.* New York: Jeremy P. Tarcher/Penguin.

The moses code. Twyman, J. F. and Walsch, N. D. (Directors). (2008).[Video/DVD] [Amsterdam]: Homescreen.

Virtue, D., (1998). *Divine guidance: How to have a dialogue with god and your guardian angels.* Los Angeles; New York: Renaissance Books; Distributed by St. Martin's Press.

Virtue, D., (1999). *Healing with the angels: How the angels can assist you in every area of your life.* Carlsbad, CA: Hay House.

Virtue, D., (2003). *Archangels & ascended masters: A guide to working and healing with divinities and deities.* Carlsbad, Calif.: Hay House.

Virtue, D., (2006). *The best of doreen virtue.* [Carlsbad, Calif.]: Hay House Audio.

Virtue, D., (2006). *Divine magic: The seven sacred secrets of manifestation: A new interpretation of the hermetic classic alchemical manual the kybalion.* Carlsbad, Calif.: Hay House.

Virtue, D., (2007). *How to hear your angels.* London: Hay House.

Virtue, D., (2011). *The healing miracles of archangel raphael.* [Carlsbad, CA]: Hay House Audio.

Virtue, D., & Lukomski, J., (2005). *Crystal therapy: How to heal and empower your life with crystal energy.* Carlsbad, Calif.: Hay House.

Virtue, D., & Virtue, C. (2009). *Signs from above: Your angels' messages about your life purpose, relationships, health, and more.* Carlsbad, Calif.: Hay House.

Walsch, N. D. (1996). *Conversations with god: An uncommon dialogue.* New York: G.P. Putnam's Sons.

Weiss, B. L. (1988). *Many lives, many masters.* New York: Simon & Schuster.

Weiss, B. L. (1992). *Through time into healing.* New York: Simon & Schuster.

Weiss, B. L. (2004). *Same soul, many bodies: Discover the healing power of future lives through progression therapy.* New York: Free Press.

Weiss, B. L. (2008). *Regression through the mirrors of time.* [Carlsbad, CA]: Hay House Audio.

Weiss, B. L., & Hay House Audio. (2008). *Regression to times and places.* [Carlsbad, Calif.]: Hay House Audio.

Weiss, B. L., & Hay House Audio. (*Through regression.* [Carlsbad, Calif.]: Hay House Audio.

Notes